THIS BOOK BELONGS TO...

SUNDERLAND A.F.C.

Name: _____ Age: _____

Favourite player: _____

2016-2017
My Predictions...   Actual...

Sunderland's final position:

Sunderland's top scorer:

Premier League Champions:

Premier League top scorer:

FA Cup Winners:

EFL Cup Winners:

Written by Rob and Barbara Mason

A TWOCAN PUBLICATION

©2016. Published by twocan under licence from Sunderland AFC.

ISBN 978-1-909872-85-1

£8

PICTURE CREDITS: Getty Images, Ian Horrocks, Alan Hewson, Barbara and Rob Mason.

CONTENTS

Goals, goals, goals. They are what the game is all about. Great saves can be spectacular and as good as a goal if the 'keeper stops the opposition scoring. Great tackles can really get the crowd going and great passing can gain control of the game and create goals but there's nothing like the ball smacking the back of the net to make the crowd erupt.

GREAT Goals

WAHBI KHAZRI v MANCHESTER UNITED

Khazri's first goal in English football saw his free kick from way out be missed by everyone in a packed penalty area and creep inside David de Gea's far post.

FABIO BORINI v CRYSTAL PALACE

What a Fab goal. Sam Allardyce thought it was the best goal scored in the Premier League all season. Right in the last minute Borini belted home a stunning equaliser with a perfectly hit pile-driver when a shot didn't even look on.

JERMAIN DEFOE v NEWCASTLE UNITED

All week leading up to the derby J.D. had been very confident of scoring – as he had on his two previous visits to St. James'. A minute before half time the Magpies flapped at a corner and as the ball dropped, which striker had read it and was perfectly placed to hit a first-time shot home? Of course, it was the 'Jer-main man.'

Sunderland have scored some crackers in 2016.

Which one is your favourite? Let's hope that in next year's annual Samson and Delilah have some even better ones to choose from!

WAHBI KHAZRI v CHELSEA

Chelsea had taken an early lead but in a vital late season game this Wahbi wonder goal got The Lads level in a match they went on to win. Khazri caught the ball brilliantly to blast the ball home and nearly burst the net!

Former Chelsea player Fabio Borini made it four goals in his last four games against the Blues in a Sunderland shirt. His powerful right foot shot was unstoppable and was The Wearsiders' second equaliser of what was a sensational afternoon.

FABIO BORINI v CHELSEA

JERMAINE DEFOE v NORWICH CITY

Sunderland's 2000th top-flight away goal was a classic clinical finish by ace poacher Defoe in what was a key win away to relegation rivals

JERMAIN DEFOE v MANCHESTER CITY

Sunderland's star striker began this season doing what he does best - terrorising Premier League defences and banging in some great goals!

JASON DENAYER
4 CENTRE-BACK

BIRTHPLACE: Brussels **BIRTHDATE:** 26/06/95

PREVIOUS CLUBS: Loans to Celtic and Galatasary.
On loan to Sunderland from Manchester City

INTERNATIONAL: Belgium

On loan to Sunderland from Manchester City, Jason is a Belgium international who has Champions League experience with Celtic and Galatasary. He became the Young Player of the year in Scotland when he did the league and cup double with Celtic while last season with Galatasary he won the Turkish cup.

MIKA
12 GOALKEEPER

FULL NAME: Michael Simoes Domingues

BIRTHPLACE: Yverden, Switzerland **BIRTHDATE:** 08/03/91

PREVIOUS CLUBS: Uniap Leiria, Benfica B, Atletico CP, Boavista

INTERNATIONAL: Portugal Under-21

Voted goalkeeper of the tournament at the 2011 FIFA Under 20 World Cup when he broke the record for minutes without conceding, saved three penalties in a shoot-out and helped Portugal to the final. Made 55 league appearances in the last two seasons with Boavista and played three times for them at the start of this season (keeping two clean sheets) before joining Sunderland on a two year deal.

THE LATEST LADS

DIDIER NDONG

17 MIDFIELD

BIRTHPLACE: Lamberene, Gabon **BIRTHDATE:** 17/06/94

PREVIOUS CLUBS: CS Sfaxien, Lorient

INTERNATIONAL: Gabon

Sunderland splashed out £13.5m to bring 22 year old Didier from the same club Lamine Kone was signed from. A hard running, mobile player, NDong is a key player for his country, Gabon (which is on the west of Africa) and in his first full season with Lorient, showed he could dominate the centre of the park.

VICTOR ANICHEBE

28 FORWARD

BIRTHPLACE: Lagos, Nigeria **BIRTHDATE:** 23/08/88

PREVIOUS CLUBS: Everton, WBA

INTERNATIONAL: Nigeria

Signed after the summer transfer window was closed, Anichebe was available as a free agent having been released by West Brom. Although he was born in Nigeria Victor grew up on Merseyside and played for David Moyes at Everton. He won a silver medal with Nigeria at the 2008 Olympics and while mainly a target man can play in a wide position or even as a holding midfielder.

BILLY JONES

2 FULL-BACK

BIRTHPLACE: Shrewsbury   BIRTHDATE: 24/03/87

PREVIOUS CLUBS: Crewe Alexandra, Preston North End, West Bromwich Albion

INTERNATIONAL: England U20

Jones is an experienced player who prefers to be on the right but can operate on the left. His versatility allows him to also play at centre back or as a defensive midfielder and he can always be relied upon to give everything he has for the cause.

VITO MANNONE

1 GOALKEEPER

BIRTHPLACE: Desio, Italy   BIRTHDATE: 02/03/88

PREVIOUS CLUBS: Atalanta, Arsenal, Barnsley (loan), Hull City (loan)

INTERNATIONAL: Italy U21

The hero of the 2014 Capital One Cup run when his penalty shoot-out saves earned victory over David Moyes' Manchester United at Old Trafford in the semi final, Mannone than played in the Wembley final on his birthday.

PATRICK VAN AANHOLT

3 LEFT-BACK

BIRTHPLACE: Den Bosch   BIRTHDATE: 03/07/88

PREVIOUS CLUBS: Chelsea, loans to Coventry City, Newcastle United, Leicester City, Wigan Athletic and Vitesse Arnhem.

INTERNATIONAL: Netherlands.

Now in his third season at Sunderland, van Aanholt did well in his first year but began his second season badly before improving so much that long before the end of the season he had become one of the team's best players. Excellent going forward and a goal threat coming in from the flank.

SUNDERLAND A.F.C.
CONSECTATIO EXCELLENTIAE

PAPY DJILOBODJI

5
DEFENDER

BIRTHPLACE: Kaolack, Senegal   **BIRTHDATE:** 01/12/88

PREVIOUS CLUBS: Chelsea, Werder Bremen (loan).

INTERNATIONAL: Senegal

Sunderland's first signing under David Moyes, Djilobodji cost £8m from Chelsea. He had been playing in Germany on loan to Werder Bremen who he helped avoid relegation last season.

PREMIER LEAGUE
SQUAD

LEE CATTERMOLE

6
MIDFIELD

BIRTHPLACE: Stockton **BIRTHDATE:** 21/03/88

PREVIOUS CLUB: Middlesbrough, Wigan Athletic

INTERNATIONAL: England Under 21

Cattermole is an energetic and committed player who is famed for his tackling but underrated as a player. He can dominate games and leads by example, always demanding the maximum from his team-mates.

SEB LARSSON

7
MIDFIELD

BIRTHPLACE: Eskilstuna, Sweden **BIRTHDATE:** 06/06/85

PREVIOUS CLUBS: Eskilstuna City, IFK Eskilstuna, Arsenal, Birmingham City

INTERNATIONAL: Sweden

Only Gianfranco Zola and Juan Mata have scored from more Premier League free-kicks that Seb Larsson. A most hard working team player Larsson has also won more international caps while on Sunderland's books than anyone else ever has, breaking the record of the great Charlie Hurley.

JACK RODWELL

8
MIDFIELD

BIRTHPLACE: Southport **BIRTHDATE:** 11/03/91

PREVIOUS CLUBS: Everton, Manchester City

INTERNATIONAL: England

A big money signing from Man City, Rodwell was given his debut by David Moyes when they were both at Everton. Signed as a box to box midfielder, Jack can also operate in defence.

WAHBI KHAZRI

10 MIDFIELD

BIRTHPLACE: Ajaccio, France **BIRTHDATE:** 08/02/91

PREVIOUS CLUBS: Bastia, Bordeaux   **INTERNATIONAL:** Tunisia

Exciting attacking midfielder or winger who likes to produce the unorthodox. Excellent with his dead ball delivery, Khazri scored his first goal from a floated free kick in a win over Manchester United and smashed the best goal Sunderland scored last season in a victory over Chelsea.

JORDAN PICKFORD

13 GOALKEEPER

BIRTHPLACE: Washington   **BIRTHDATE:** 07/03/94

PREVIOUS CLUBS: Loans to, Darlington, Alfreton Town, Burton Albion, Carlisle United, Bradford City and Preston North End

INTERNATIONAL: England Under 21

Exceptional young goalkeeper who is agile, a brilliant reflex stopper and has distribution as good as any 'keeper. After bagging plenty of experience on numerous loans, 'Pickers' made his debut for Sunderland early in 2016 and hopes to become number one in 2016-17.

FABIO BORINI

9 FORWARD

BIRTHPLACE: Bentivoglio, Emilia-Romagna, Italy

BIRTHDATE: 29/03/91

PREVIOUS CLUB: Chelsea, Swansea City, Liverpool, Roma,   **INTERNATIONAL:** Italy

Scored for Sunderland at Wembley against Manchester City in the 2014 Capital One Cup final, Fabio is a man for the big occasion. He has come up with some important and spectacular goals for Sunderland.

SUNDERLAND A.F.C.

CONSECRATIO EXCELLENTIAE

DUNCAN WATMORE

14
FORWARD

BIRTHPLACE: Manchester **BIRTHDATE:** 08/03/94

PREVIOUS CLUBS: Manchester United, Altrincham, Clitheroe (loan), Curzon Ashton (loan), Hibs (loan).

INTERNATIONAL: England Under 21

'Roadrunner' Watmore is a real danger with his direct running. He puts defences under pressure with his pace and is always likely to score or create a chance. Has a particular understanding with goalkeeper Pickford for club and country, the pair being born a day apart.

JOHN O'SHEA

16
DEFENDER

BIRTHPLACE: Waterford **BIRTHDATE:** 30/04/81

PREVIOUS CLUBS: Waterford Bohemians, Manchester United, Royal Antwerp (loan), Bournemouth (loan)

INTERNATIONAL: Republic of Ireland

Vastly experienced versatile player who won trophies galore at Manchester United before joining Sunderland in 2011 and going on to play over 150 games for SAFC who he captained in the 2014 Capital One Cup final. Damaged ligaments after two games of this season ruled him out for the first part of the season.

JERMAIN DEFOE

18
STRIKER

BIRTHPLACE: Becton, London **BIRTHDATE:** 07/02/82

PREVIOUS CLUB: Charlton Athletic, West Ham United, Bournemouth (loan), Tottenham Hotspur, Portsmouth, Tottenham Hotspur (second spell), Toronto Blizzard.

INTERNATIONAL: England

Sunderland's Player of the Year, 'J.D' top scored last season with 18 goals in all competitions including two hat-tricks. He is a top class player who has become a big hero on Wearside.

NEW Boy

PADDY McNAIR

19 MIDFIELD

BIRTHPLACE: Ballyclare **BIRTHDATE:** 27/04/95

PREVIOUS CLUBS: Manchester United

INTERNATIONAL: Northern Ireland

Having played 24 times for Manchester United in the last two seasons, Paddy played twice at the summer's European Championships, for Northern Ireland including the historic victory over Ukraine.

STEVEN PIENAAR

20
MIDFIELD

BIRTHPLACE: Westbury, South Africa   **BIRTHDATE:** 17/03/82

PREVIOUS CLUBS: Ajax Cape Town, Ajax, Borussia Dortmund, Everton, Tottenham Hotspur, Everton (second spell).

INTERNATIONAL: South Africa

Formerly with David Moyes at Everton, veteran Steven Pienaar joined Sunderland on a one year deal a couple of days before his debut against Middlesbrough. Providing quality on the ball, Pienaar played at the 2010 World Cup when his country was the host nation.

NEW Boy

NEW Boy

JAVIER MANQUILLO

21
RIGHT-BACK

BIRTHPLACE: Madrid **BIRTHDATE:** 05/05/94

PREVIOUS CLUBS: Atletico Madrid, Liverpool (loan) Marseille (loan)

INTERNATIONAL: Spain Under 21

Talented right back brought in on a season long loan from Atletico Madrid having been on loan to Marseille in the previous campaign, when he was a team mate of Steven Fletcher who was on loan from Sunderland. Earlier in his career Manquillo had been on loan to Liverpool and for both of his English clubs he debuted against Southampton.

NEW Boy

DONALD LOVE **22** FULL-BACK

BIRTHPLACE: Rochdale   BIRTHDATE: 02/12/94

PREVIOUS CLUBS: Northwich Town, Manchester United, Wigan Athletic (loan)

INTERNATIONAL: Scotland U21

Made his Premier League debut for Manchester United at the Stadium of Light in February of 2016 and moved to Sunderland six months later. English born but qualifies for Scotland through his grandmother.

LAMINE KONE

BIRTHPLACE: Paris **BIRTHDATE:** 01/02/89

PREVIOUS CLUBS: Chateaureux, Lorient

INTERNATIONAL: Ivory Coast

Powerfully dominant centre back, Kone quickly became a crowd favourite after joining in January and became the first central defender to scorer twice in a top flight game for Sunderland in over 100 years when he did so in the win over Everton which guaranteed Sunderland's place in the Premier League this season.

JAN KIRCHHOFF

27 MIDFIELD

BIRTHPLACE: Frankfurt **BIRTHDATE:** 01/10/90

PREVIOUS CLUBS: Mainz, Bayern Munich, Schalke (loan)

INTERNATIONAL: Germany U21

A defensive midfielder or centre-back, Jan performed fantastically for Sunderland last season after arriving for a bargain fee of under £1m in January. Troubled by injury earlier in his career, Kirchhoff's quality is genuinely top class.

SUNDERLAND A.F.C.

JOEL ASORO — 29 STRIKER

BIRTHPLACE: Osterharinge, Sweden   **BIRTHDATE:** 27/04/99

PREVIOUS CLUB: Bromma, (Sweden)   **INTERNATIONAL:** Sweden Under 21

Highly rated Sweden youth international forward forcing himself into the first team picture, scoring for the first team in pre-season, becoming Sunderland's youngest Premier League player when he debuted as a sub against Middlesbrough and making a first start against Shrewsbury Town.

Last season scored seven goals at under 18 level from nine starts with a further five appearances off the bench.

LYNDEN GOOCH — 46 STRIKER

BIRTHPLACE: Santa Cruz, California   **BIRTHDATE:** 24.12.95

PREVIOUS CLUB: None   **INTERNATIONAL:** USA U23

Made his Premier League debut on the first day of this season at Manchester City. Played 10 games on loan to Doncaster last season after making his Sunderland debut in the Capital One Cup. USA U23 international who has an English mother and Irish father.

NEW Boy

ADNAN JANUZAJ **44** WINGER

BIRTHPLACE: Brussels **BIRTHDATE:** 05/02/95

PREVIOUS CLUBS: FC Brussels, Anderlecht, Manchester United, Borussia Dortmund (loan)

INTERNATIONAL: Belgium

On a year's loan from Manchester United, Adnan made his debut for The Red Devils at Wembley in the 2013 Charity Shield against Wigan and scored twice at Sunderland later that year on his first start.

DAVID MOYES THE PLAYER

David Moyes played for:

IBV - a club in Iceland where he played in the youth team

DRUMCHAPEL AMATEURS	CELTIC
CAMBRIDGE UNITED	BRISTOL CITY
SHREWSBURY TOWN	DUNFERMLINE ATHLETIC
HAMILTON ACADEMICAL	PRESTON NORTH END

Big Sam was a top class manager but David Moyes' record is even better - only Sir Alex Ferguson has been Manager of the Year as many times as him, Sir Alex winning the award four times to David's three with only Arsene Wenger and Steve Coppell winning it twice. Earlier in his career Moyes also won divisional manager of the year awards in back to back seasons with Preston who he took to promotion and the Play Offs.

He qualified for the Champions League and reached the FA Cup final with Everton and reached the quarter final of the Champions League and semi final of the League Cup with Manchester United while with Real Sociedad Moyes masterminded a sensational win over Barcelona.

DAVID MOYES FACT FILE

- He has the fourth highest number of Premier League wins as a manager.
- He has been Manager of the Year three times: in 2003, 2005 and 2009.
- When he was appointed at Sunderland he had also been Manager of the Month 10 times.
- At Sunderland he replaced Sam Allardyce. When David Moyes played for Preston, Allardyce was Preston's youth team coach.
- When he became Preston's manager, David Moyes got them promoted to what is now the Championship and then reached the Play Offs as North End got close to the Premier League.
- After winning 113 games and losing only 63 with Preston, Mr. Moyes became manager of Everton in March 2002.
- Everton qualified for the Champions League by finishing fourth in 2005.
- Everton qualified for the UEFA Cup in 2007. That competition is now called The Europa League.
- In 2008 Everton finished fifth and reached the League Cup semi-final.
- In 2009 Everton reached the FA Cup final and qualified for the Europa League.
- From 2010 to 2013 The Toffees finished 8th, 7th, 7th and 6th.
- In 2013 he took over as manager of Manchester United winning the Community Shield at Wembley.
- During his season there Manchester United reached the semi final of the Capital One Cup – losing on penalties to…Sunderland.
- My Moyes also guided Manchester United to the quarter final of the Champions League.
- In November 2014 he became manager of Real Sociedad in Spain staying there for a day short of a year. The highlight of his time in la Liga was Real Sociedad upsetting the odds by beating Barcelona.

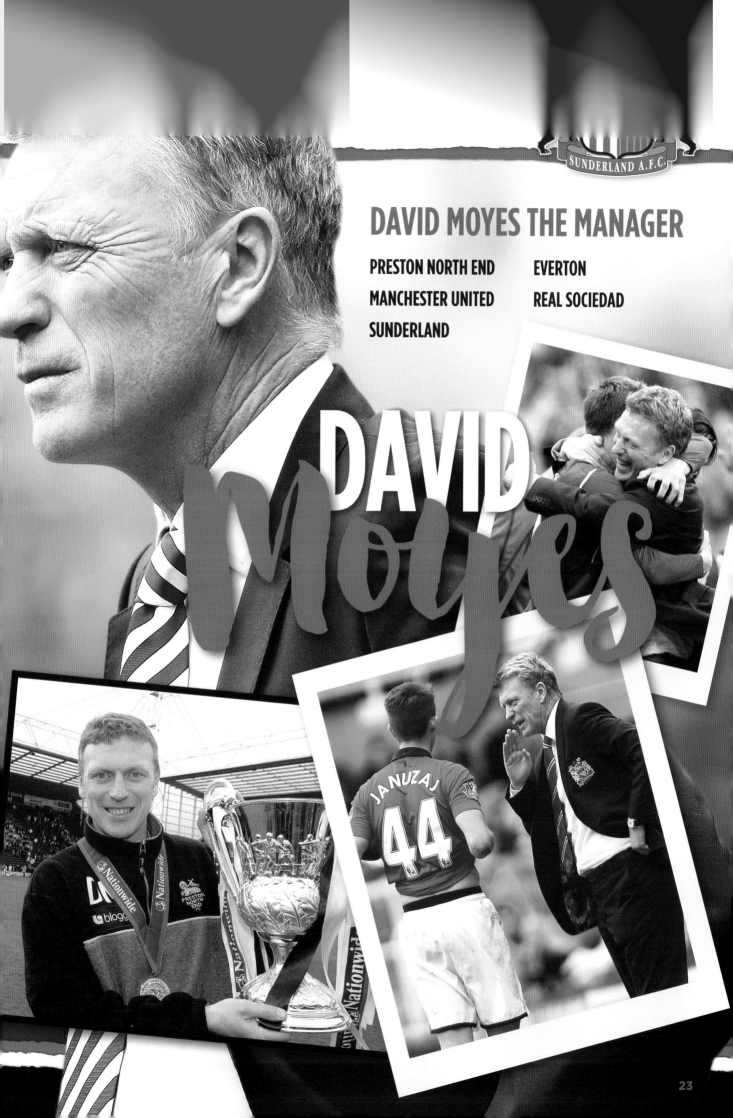

DAVID MOYES THE MANAGER

PRESTON NORTH END   **EVERTON**

MANCHESTER UNITED   **REAL SOCIEDAD**

SUNDERLAND

DAVID *Moyes*

CUP FINAL CAPTAINS

Bobby Kerr was the smallest man to ever raise the FA Cup.

At 5'4" 'The Little General' captained Sunderland in what was the biggest upset in the history of the FA Cup.

In 1973 opponents Leeds United were the most powerful team in the country. Full of top class players Leeds and with a European final against AC Milan to come soon after, Leeds were the hottest favourites in years.

Sunderland were in the second division at the time and just six months earlier had even been near the bottom of that league. However new manager Bob Stokoe (His statue is now outside the Stadium of Light) took over and turned the team into a one that played without fear.

Midfielder Kerr was one of several really good players Sunderland had. Centre half Dave Watson and forward Dennis Tueart went on to play for England and goalie Jim Montgomery showed his great ability by making the best save ever seen at Wembley in the final.

The skipper was one of four Scots in the side. Full back Dick Malone marked Leeds' danger-man Eddie Gray out of the game, skilful midfielder Ian Porterfield scored the only game of the game from a corner taken by Billy Hughes who went on to be capped by Scotland. The corner was won when Leeds 'keeper David Harvey tipped over a cross-shot from Kerr.

Six years before lifting the cup Bobby Kerr had broken his leg against Leeds in the FA Cup. Kerr was still a teenager when he burst onto the scene on the last day of 1966 when he scored the only goal of the game against Manchester City. Young Bobby had scored seven goals in his first 11 games when he broke his leg but fought back and went on to play over 400 games for the team he captained to cup triumph.

1973

BOBBY
Keri

CAN YOU WIN THE *League*

GET YOUR KIT READY

To play this game you need to get a dice (a die is its proper name) and a different coloured counter for everyone who wants to play. If you don't have any counters just use a different coin for every player.

REFEREE

You'll need a referee. Sometimes you have to answer questions to move forward.
The answers are on page 62 so you'll need someone who isn't playing to be able to check the answers.

KICK OFF

To start you have to roll a three to move forward the first three places.
The youngest player gets to roll the dice first, second youngest second and so on.

PENALTY APPEAL

If you roll a six when any of your opponents are on square 30 or above you can appeal for a penalty. If you do then the person who is nearly at the end has to roll the dice three times. If the combined total of their three rolls of the dice doesn't come to 10 or more they have to move back to the same square number as the person who has made the penalty appeal.

FINAL WHISTLE

The winner is the first player to reach the final square having got past all of the obstacles.

9

10

15

16

21 Go forward one square for every one of the three teams relegated from the Premier League last season that you can name.

22

3

35

1

2

3

4

5

6 Have another roll of the dice in honour of the '6 in a row' derby run

7 Miss a turn

8

1

12

13 Prove 13 isn't unlucky by telling every other player to go back to square 3!

14

17

18

19 Miss a turn if you can't name the Black Cats' number 19

20

23

24 Sing the Match of the Day tune to be able to make whoever is in the lead go back to square three

25

26

28 Name the year SAFC last won the FA Cup to get an extra turn

29

30

32 If you know which Premier League team Jermain Defoe scored a hat-trick against last season you can have two extra turns.

33

34 Name the Sunderland star who played for the Republic of Ireland at the Euro's last summer or miss a turn.

36

37 Miss a turn

38

The Stadium of Light...

England AT THE SOL

...is one of the best and most modern grounds in the country.

Along with Manchester City's Etihad Stadium and Wembley, Sunderland's home was used by England for one of their three warm up games just before the European Championships.

Australia were the visitors in front of a sold out crowd of over 46,000 who saw Manchester United's Marcus Rashford score within three minutes of making his first start in an England jersey.

When Rashford's club mate Wayne Rooney spectacularly extended his tally as England's record goal-scorer Roy Hodgson's side looked like they might go on to score a few more goals but they had to settle for a 2-1 win after Tottenham's Eric Dier put through his own goal.

It was the third time England have played a full international at the Stadium of Light and they made it three wins out of three having also beaten Turkey and Belgium in previous games at what is the most northerly stadium in the Premier League.

It was tremendous to have The Three Lions at the home of The Black Cats and Australia were very welcome visitors, the Aussies even using the Academy of Light as their training base.

Frank Lampard, England 2-1 Belgium, 1999

David Beckham, England 2-0 Turkey, 2003

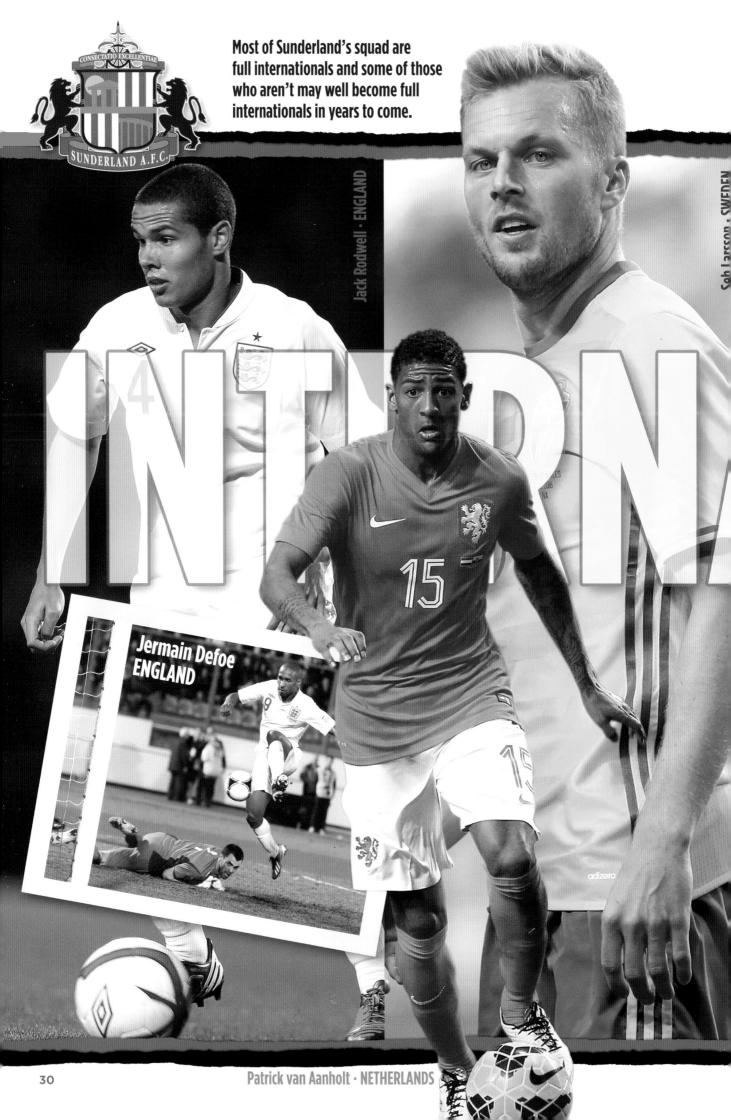

Most of Sunderland's squad are full internationals and some of those who aren't may well become full internationals in years to come.

Jack Rodwell · ENGLAND

Seb Larsson · SWEDEN

INTERNA

Jermain Defoe
ENGLAND

Patrick van Aanholt · NETHERLANDS

England of course played at the Stadium of Light in the summer of 2016 and the national side came calling again a few weeks later when Sunderland manager Sam Allardyce became manager of the national side.

Whenever you come to see Sunderland the red and white line up is likely to include several players who also play international football.

Wahbi Khazri · TUNISIA

Papy Djilobodji · SENEGAL

NATIONAL

RED & WHITES

Fabio Borini · ITALY

Lamine Kone · IVORY COAST

John O'Shea · REPUBLIC OF IRELAND

PUZZLE PAGE

TRANSFER TRAIL

Can you name these Sunderland players from the list of clubs they have played for?

Bastia **Bordeaux** Sunderland	**West Ham** **Bournemouth** **Spurs** **Portsmouth** Toronto	**Chelsea** Coventry **Newcastle** Leicester **Wigan** Vitesse Arnhem

JUMBLE SALE

Sunderland sold this player last season. Can you work out who it is from the jumbled up letters of his name:

BIG MATCH!

Can you match the right club with the right nickname?

THE TIGERS · THE CHERRIES · THE FOXES · THE SAINTS · THE POTTERS
THE BLADES · THE OWLS · THE HORNETS · THE BLACK CATS

Can you match the right team with the right ground?

STAMFORD BRIDGE · SELHURST PARK · THE HAWTHORNS · WHITE HART LANE
ANFIELD · STADIUM OF LIGHT · GOODISON PARK · VICTORIA PARK · OLD TRAFFORD

ANSWERS ON PAGE 6

Samson's Sums

Delilah likes to make sure Samson tries hard with his sums.

Can you help him work them out?

1 DJILOBODJI + DEFOE = ◯

2 CATTERMOLE + LARSSON = ◯

3 GOOCH + JANUZAJ = ◯

4 KIRCHHOFF − RODWELL = ◯

5 LOVE − McNAIR = ◯

6 O'SHEA − WATMORE = ◯

7 BORINI X VAN AANHOLT = ◯

8 PICKFORD X KHAZRI = ◯

9 O'SHEA ÷ RODWELL = ◯

10 JANUZAJ + DEFOE X

JONES ÷ DENAYER = ◯

1	Vito Mannone
2	Billy Jones
3	Patrick van Aanholt
4	Jason Denayer
5	Papy Djilobodji
6	Lee Cattermole
7	Seb Larsson
8	Jack Rodwell
9	Fabio Borini
10	Wahbi Khazri
12	Mika
13	Jordan Pickford
14	Duncan Watmore
16	John O'Shea
17	Didier Ndong
18	Jermain Defoe
19	Paddy McNair
20	Steven Pienaar
22	Donald Love
23	Lamine Kone
25	Ethan Robson
27	Jan Kirchhoff
28	Victor Anichebe
29	Joel Asoro
31	Thomas Beadling
32	Max Stryjek
34	Tommy Robson
35	Josh Maja
37	Rees Greenwood
39	George Honeyman
43	Michael Ledger
44	Adnan Januzaj
45	Josh Robson
46	Lynden Gooch

How did you get on?

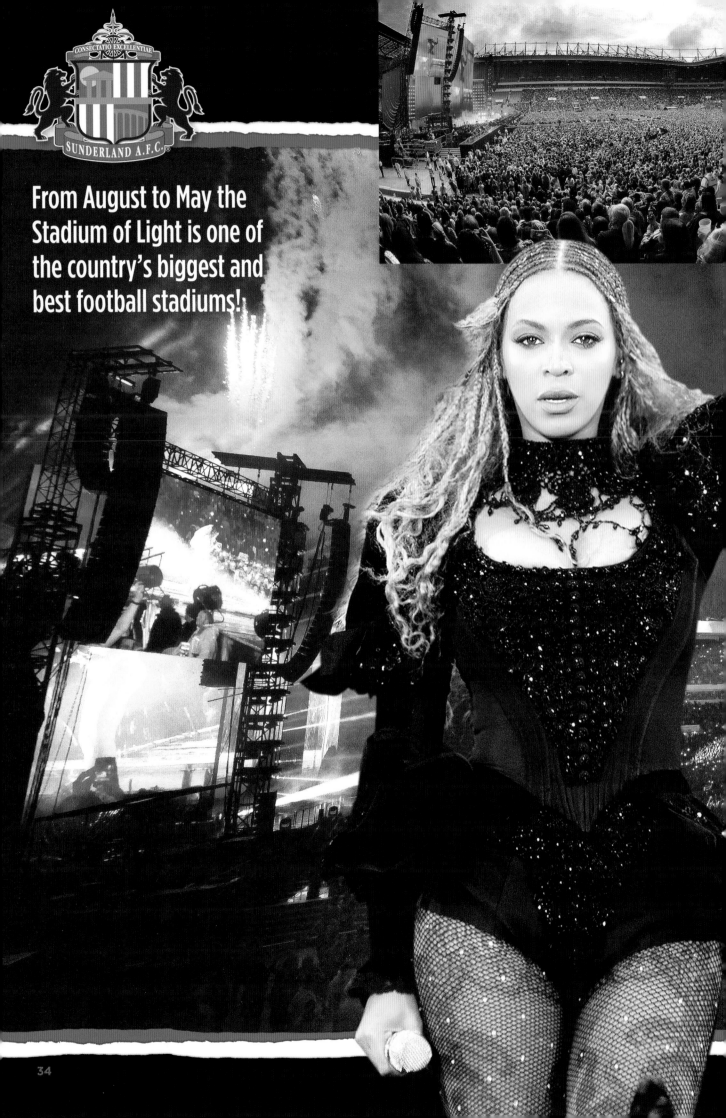

From August to May the Stadium of Light is one of the country's biggest and best football stadiums!

Even England played there in their last match outside Wembley before heading off to the Euro's, but in the summer. the Stadium of Light becomes the north-east's premier place for the biggest stars in the world of music.

Beyonce

Beyonce put on a stunning show of over two hours.

It was the opening night of Queen Bey's European tour with many of the songs from her album Lemonade, but there were the great hits of the past too as she thrilled the capacity crowd with a spectacular show dominated by a gigantic four sided video screen that revolved as Beyonce and her 14 dancers strutted their stuff.

One Direction, Take That, Oasis, Rihanna and Coldplay are just some of the superstars to play at the Stadium of Light in recent years. Wonder who'll be added to that list in the next few years? Will it be your favourites?

This year it was Beyonce who turned on the style in front of over 50,000 fans who came to see the American superstar.

LADIES

Tori Williams

Sunderland Ladies have played their games in the summer since 2014 when they joined the FA Women's Super League.

In 2017 though there are going to be big changes as the Ladies game will change from a summer season to a winter season like the men's game.

Between the 2016 WSL season finishing in November and the 2017-18 campaign starting in September 2017 the Ladies team will take part in a special one-off competition.

SPRING SERIES

To fill in the gap between the last summer season and the first winter season Sunderland Ladies will play in a tournament called The Spring Series between February and June. WSL 1 teams will play from 22 April to 3 June while WSL 2 teams will be in action in their Spring Series from 11 February to 20 May.

In this competition teams in the league will all play each other but just once rather than playing each other home and away. Once the Spring Series is over England players will take part in the Euro's before the WSL starts again with its new Winter look.

SAFC

CHANGING SEASONS

WINTER WSL

The winter WSL once it gets going will have two divisions. There will be ten teams in the top flight wit` eleven at the lower level.

Although it is a winter season there will be a winter break from the middle of December to the middle of January so next Christmas there'll be plenty of time for the Ladies team to read their new SAFC annual!

After the winter break the season will carry on until May.

Stephanie ROCHE

Lucy STANIFORTH

Victoria WILLIAMS

SUNDERLAND A.F.C.

JAKE HACKETT

BIRTHPLACE: Durham
POSITION: Midfield
AGE WHEN JOINING THE SUNDERLAND ACADEMY: 8
BIGGEST INFLUENCE ON CAREER SO FAR: My dad
Solid tackler with a good range of passing.

JORDAN HICKEY

BIRTHPLACE: Sunderland
POSITION: Midfield/Defence
AGE WHEN JOINING THE SUNDERLAND ACADEMY: 11
BIGGEST INFLUENCE ON CAREER SO FAR: My family
Versatile and determined player who is an excellent tackler and has the ability to drill accurate long diagonal balls.

BENJAMIN KIMPIOKA

BIRTHPLACE: Uppsala, Sweden
AGE WHEN JOINING THE SUNDERLAND ACADEMY: 16
POSITION: Winger or striker
BIGGEST INFLUENCE ON CAREER SO FAR: My brother.
Willowy winger who is all arms and legs as he torments defenders who never know what he going to do next.

LEE CONNELLY

BIRTHPLACE: Glasgow   **POSITION:** Striker
AGE WHEN JOINING THE SUNDERLAND ACADEMY: 16
BIGGEST INFLUENCE ON CAREER SO FAR: My dad
Diminutive hard worker with a real eye for goal. Played for Scotland at the Under 17 European Championships last summer and won his first U19 caps in September.

FERGUS McAUGHTRIE

BIRTHPLACE: York
AGE WHEN JOINING THE SUNDERLAND ACADEMY: 15
POSITION: Left back
BIGGEST INFLUENCE ON CAREER SO FAR: Mum & Dad
Good dribbler who likes to get forward and support his attack.

JACK CONNOLLY

BIRTHPLACE: Dublin, Ireland
POSITION: Centre midfield
AGE WHEN JOINING THE SUNDERLAND ACADEMY: 16
POSITION: Centre midfield
BIGGEST INFLUENCE ON CAREER SO FAR: My dad

ANTHONY PATTERSON

BIRTHPLACE: Newcastle
AGE WHEN JOINING THE SUNDERLAND ACADEMY: 9
POSITION: Goalkeeper
Unlucky to be injured at the start of the season.

JACK DIAMOND

BIRTHPLACE: Gateshead
POSITION: Attacking midfielder
AGE WHEN JOINING THE SUNDERLAND ACADEMY: 13
BIGGEST INFLUENCE ON CAREER SO FAR: My family
Skilful player who can rip up defences on the wing or play through the middle as a striker.

JACOB YOUNG

BIRTHPLACE: Wallongong, Australia.
AGE WHEN JOINING THE SUNDERLAND ACADEMY: 15
POSITION: Centre back
BIGGEST INFLUENCE ON CAREER SO FAR: My dad and a previous coach, Mark Lee.
Tall defender who is difficult to beat in the air.

SECOND YEARS

They are coached by **Elliott Dickman and Mark Atkinson** who are both former Sunderland AFC youth players themselves.

OWEN GAMBLE

BIRTHPLACE: Worksop **POSITION:** Centre midfield
AGE WHEN JOINING THE SUNDERLAND ACADEMY: 15
BIGGEST INFLUENCE ON CAREER SO FAR: My granddad and dad
U18 STARTS LAST SEASON: 19 **GOALS LAST SEASON:** 0
UNDER 18 SUBSTITUTE APPEARANCES LAST SEASON: 6

OSCAR KRUSNELL

BIRTHPLACE: Stockholm, Sweden **POSITION:** Left back
AGE WHEN JOINING THE SUNDERLAND ACADEMY: 16
BIGGEST INFLUENCE ON CAREER SO FAR: My dad
U18 STARTS LAST SEASON: 6 **GOALS LAST SEASON:** 0
UNDER 18 SUBSTITUTE APPEARANCES LAST SEASON: 5
Sweden youth international who defends well and is capable of crossing well when he gets forward.

JOSH MAJA

BIRTHPLACE: Lewisham **POSITION:** Striker
AGE WHEN JOINING THE SUNDERLAND ACADEMY: 16
BIGGEST INFLUENCE ON CAREER SO FAR: My mum
U18 STARTS LAST SEASON: 15 **GOALS LAST SEASON:** 8
UNDER 18 SUBSTITUTE APPEARANCES LAST SEASON: 4
Skilful player capable of producing spectacular moments. Likely to feature in the first team squad this season.

ALEX STOREY

BIRTHPLACE: Hetton **POSITION:** Centre back
AGE WHEN JOINING THE SUNDERLAND ACADEMY: 7
BIGGEST INFLUENCE ON CAREER SO FAR: My dad
U18 STARTS LAST SEASON: 24 **GOALS LAST SEASON:** 1
UNDER 18 SUBSTITUTE APPEARANCES LAST SEASON: 1
Commanding centre half who is a local lad that attended Hetton School.

CHRIS ALLAN

BIRTHPLACE: Jarrow **POSITION:** Centre midfield
AGE WHEN JOINING THE SUNDERLAND ACADEMY: 7
U18 STARTS LAST SEASON: 2 **GOALS LAST SEASON:** 0
UNDER 18 SUBSTITUTE APPEARANCES LAST SEASON: 4
Physically strong player for whom this is a big season after injury problems have held him back in the past.

BRANDON TAYLOR

BIRTHPLACE: Gateshead **POSITION:** Right/Centre back
AGE WHEN JOINING THE SUNDERLAND ACADEMY: 11
BIGGEST INFLUENCE ON CAREER SO FAR: My parents.
U18 STARTS LAST SEASON: 12 **GOALS LAST SEASON:** 0
UNDER 18 SUBSTITUTE APPEARANCES LAST SEASON: 1
Composed and versatile defender looking to progress further this season.

ADAM BALE

BIRTHPLACE: Manchester **POSITION:** Centre midfield
AGE WHEN JOINING THE SUNDERLAND ACADEMY: 13
BIGGEST INFLUENCE ON CAREER SO FAR: My mum
U18 STARTS LAST SEASON: 10 **GOALS LAST SEASON:** 0
UNDER 18 SUBSTITUTE APPEARANCES LAST SEASON: 4
Good organiser who is very vocal on the pitch. Determined ball winner who links play well.

MICHAEL WOUD

BIRTHPLACE: Auckland, New Zealand
AGE WHEN JOINING THE SUNDERLAND ACADEMY: 16
POSITION: Goalkeeper **U18 STARTS LAST SEASON:** 10
BIGGEST INFLUENCE ON CAREER SO FAR: My parents
UNDER 18 SUBSTITUTE APPEARANCES LAST SEASON: 0
Played for New Zealand at the U17 World Cup in Chile last season and in the U20 World Cup qualifying games in September.

U23s

SUNDERLAND UNDER 23s PLAY IN PREMIER LEAGUE 2

They also compete in the Checkatrade Trophy, Premier League Cup and Premier League International Cup.

DAN CASEY
BIRTHDATE: 29.10.97
BIRTHPLACE: Dublin
POSITION: Centre back who can play full back
FACT: Republic of Ireland youth international who is a commanding and mightily determined defender. Can also play as a full back.

ELLIOT EMBLETON
BIRTHDATE: 02.04.99
BIRTHPLACE: Durham
POSITION: Midfield
FACT: Highly talented England player who scored the Under 23s first goal of this season from the penalty spot in a pre-season game at Seaham.

REES GREENWOOD
BIRTHDATE: 10.12.96
BIRTHPLACE: Newcastle   **POSITION:** Winger
FACT: A Barclays U21 League Player of the Month award, an England U20 debut and a Premier League debut all happened for Rees in the first half of 2016. Quite a hat-trick for a player who has been at the club since he was eight.

THOMAS BEADLING
BIRTHDATE: 16.01.96
BIRTHPLACE: Barrow   **POSITION:** Centre back
FACT: Played for Australia at Under 13 level after emigrating there. Previously at Sunderland's academy from the ages of eight to 12, he has since returned to England and progressed through the academy.

GEORGE HONEYMAN
BIRTHDATE: 08.09.94
BIRTHPLACE: Hexham   **POSITION:** Midfield
FACT: George made his Premier League debut at Watford last season after being on loan to Gateshead. He is a skilful player with an eye for a cute, defence splitting pass.

JORDAN BLINCO
BIRTHDATE: 04.12.96 **BIRTHPLACE:** Meadowsfield
POSITION: Versatile but mainly plays striker.
FACT: Jordan spent the final part of last season playing on loan in Norway with Bergsoy. Joined SAFC in 2015 after previously being with Darlington. In 2014-15 he was top scorer for Sunderland at Under 18 level and has also had loan experience with Boston.

DENVER HUME
BIRTHDATE: 11.8.98
BIRTHPLACE: Ashington
POSITION: Left back
FACT: Played in more Under 18 games than anyone else last season (28) but began this season with an injury.

GEORGE BRADY
BIRTHDATE: 29.12.96 **BIRTHPLACE:** Gassin, France
POSITION: Centre back
FACT: George is a former Chelsea defender and part of a 'Brady bunch' that includes aunt Karren Vice-Chairman at West Ham and Grandad Terry, a former director of Portsmouth and chairman of Swindon Town.

CARL LAWSON
BIRTHDATE: 01.10.94
BIRTHPLACE: Sunderland
POSITION: Striker or midfield
FACT: Attacking player who lost best part of a year to injury earlier in his career but who is now looking to make a sustained impression.

They are coached by Elliott Dickman and Cliff Byrne.

MICHAEL LEDGER

BIRTHDATE: 15.11.96 **BIRTHPLACE:** Shotley Bridge
POSITION: Centre back
FACT: With the club since he was eight, Michael captained the Under 18s. A former season ticket holder, he is developing physically at a rapid rate and featured at first team level in pre-season.

ETHAN ROBSON

BIRTHDATE: 25.10.96
BIRTHPLACE: Sunderland **POSITION:** Midfield
FACT: Signed a new contract in April after playing 90 minutes of a Behind Closed Doors first team Friendly against Scottish team Livingston at the Stadium of Light. Has been at the club since he was eight.

LUKE MOLYNEUX

BIRTHDATE: 29.03.98 **POSITION:** Winger
BIRTHPLACE: Bishop Auckland
FACT: Scored seven times in 27+2 appearances for the under 18s last season. A talented winger who has a welcome habit of scoring spectacular goals.

JOSH ROBSON

BIRTHDATE: 03.02.98
BIRTHPLACE: Harrogate **POSITION:** Right back
FACT: Got on the first team bench for the first time last season in the Capital One Cup when he was just 17 and started at first team level in the pre-season win at Rotherham. With SAFC since U10 level. Debuted for the U21s against West Ham a month after his 17th birthday.

ANDREW NELSON

BIRTHDATE: 16.09.97
BIRTHPLACE: Newton Aycliffe **POSITION:** Striker
FACT: Local lad who scored against Middlesbrough on his Under 18 debut in November 2013. He scored 11 times at that level last season and deserved every one of them for his whole-hearted industry and commitment.

TOMMY ROBSON

BIRTHDATE: 11.09.95
BIRTHPLACE: Stanley **POSITION:** Left back
FACT: Played more than anyone for the Under 21s last season and then played the full 90 minutes of the game on his Premier League debut at Watford in May. Started his career at Darlington.

OLIVER PAIN

BIRTHDATE: 28.10.97
BIRTHPLACE: Australia **POSITION:** Goalkeeper
FACT: Oliver spent two years with Crystal Palace and played for them against Real Madrid at Under 17 level before joining Sunderland in August 2016.

MAX STRYJEK

BIRTHDATE: 18.07.96
BIRTHPLACE: Warsaw, Poland **POSITION:** Goalkeeper
FACT: Max has played international football up to U20 level, has gained senior experience on loan to non-league Boston and been on the bench for Sunderland. Joined SAFC in 2013 having begun in Poland with MKS Polonia. His older brother Bartlomiej is a centre forward with Polish outfit Swit NDM.

JEAN-YVES POAME

BIRTHDATE: 15.08.98
BIRTHPLACE: Ivory Coast **POSITION:** Midfield
FACT: At Sunderland since under 15 level having previously been with a club called Carduff in Dublin. Jean-Yves is an attacking player who is a Republic of Ireland youth international.

JAMES TALBOT

BIRTHDATE: 24.04.97
BIRTHPLACE: Dublin **POSITION:** Goalkeeper
FACT: The Republic of Ireland's Player of the Year for his age group in 2013, James gained Northern League experience on loan to Sunderland RCA last season. An outstanding shot-stopper who is quick off his line and a great communicator.

DAN PYBUS

BIRTHDATE: 12.12.97
BIRTHPLACE: Newcastle **POSITION:** Midfield
FACT: An England youth international, Dan was top scorer for the Under 18s last season with 15 goals from 26 games. His dad was a professional footballer.

DAN WRIGHT

BIRTHDATE: 04.01.98
BIRTHPLACE: South Shields **POSITION:** Midfield
FACT: Dan is in his first year as a professional footballer. He has played for England up to Under 19 level. He is a tidy player who likes to knit play together in the middle of the park.

1913 CUP FINAL

Thomson was a tough player who in the cup final had such a battle with Villa centre forward Harry Hampton that the pair of them were suspended for the start of the following season.

Wembley Stadium didn't exist in 1913 when the final was played at Crystal Palace (Not Selhurst Park where Crystal Palace play now). Over 120,000 people crammed in to watch the final. Only at the first Wembley final 10 years later have more people ever watched a football match in England.

Oddly when Sunderland were in their next cup final in 1937 they had another Scotsman also called Charlie Thomson but he was not related.

The original Charlie Thomson did have cup winner's medals to his name. Before signing for Sunderland he had experienced three Scottish Cup finals for Hearts, winning two of them.

The year was 1913 and Sunderland lost 1–0 to Aston Villa. However Sunderland won the league championship in the same season, leaving Aston Villa in second place.

CHARLIE Thomson

Charlie Thomson was a Scotland international centre-half who captained Sunderland in their first FA Cup final over a century ago.

Paul first came to Sunderland in 1983 when he was signed by Alan Durban, the manager who had given him his league debut for Stoke. After a year in the north-east 'Brace' left for Everton where he won the league and the European Cup Winners' Cup as well as playing for England. He was badly hit by injuries though and returned to Sunderland where he played from 1989 until leaving after the 1992 final.

Next stop was Newcastle where he won promotion before coming back to Sunderland in 1995, this time as player/assistant manager to Peter Reid who he had played alongside at Everton. He stayed for two years before joining Fulham who he went on to manage before going on to also manage Walsall and Halifax.

In 2013 Paul came back to Sunderland to work with the academy before becoming first team coach and then assistant manager again.

PAUL Bracewell

Paul Bracewell captained Sunderland in the 1992 FA Cup final when second division Sunderland lost 2-0 to Liverpool at Wembley.

It was the fourth time Bracewell had played in an FA Cup final but unfortunately he had been a runner up on the other three occasions with Everton too.

Samson and Delilah are also the mascots of The Junior Black Cats.

DID YOU KNOW THAT IT IS FREE TO BECOME A MEMBER OF THE JUNIOR BLACK CATS?

Hopefully you are already a Junior Black Cat, but if not why not sign up for Samson and Delilah?

By being a Junior Black Cat you might get the chance to be a mascot for Sunderland. At every home game one lucky Junior Black Cat member gets the chance to be a mascot. These lucky people are chosen at random by Samson and Delilah and it could be you... if you are a member.

As well as having the chance of maybe being picked out by Samson and Delilah as a mascot by being a Junior Black Cat member you also get:

- **A membership card**
- **A Christmas card from the players**
- **A magazine sent to you three times a year.**
- **Emails from Samson**
- **Your own Junior Black Cats section on safc.com**
- **The opportunity to attend the Junior Black Cats Christmas party.**
- **The chance to come to the Junior Black Cats summer fun day**

MEMBERS MAGAZINES

Samson and Delilah produce three different magazines.

The youngest members (those aged three and under) receive a colouring book. Members aged from four to 11 have their own Junior Black Cats Magazine while older members aged from 12 to 16 get Black Cats Life.

Junior Black Cats and Black Cat Life magazine come together, so in fact you get both magazines if you are four or over so that's twice the fun.

If you live in England, Scotland, Wales or Northern Ireland you have your magazine posted three times a year and if you live outside the UK you are sent a digital version.

SIGN FOR
SAMSON & DELILAH

If you are not already a member you can join at SAFC/juniorblackcats

You can also call 0191 551 5157
or email juniorblackcats@safc.com

Make sure you ask an adult before joining.

SON & DELILAH

junior
blackcats

THE OFFICIAL SAFC JUNIOR SUPPORTERS' CLUB

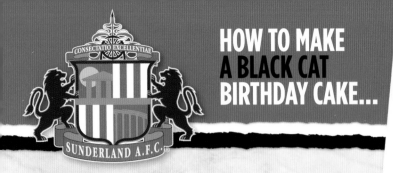

HOW TO MAKE A BLACK CAT BIRTHDAY CAKE...

YOU WILL NEED:

- Permission to start creating in the kitchen!
- 200 gm caster sugar
- 200 gm self-raising flour
- 4 large eggs
- 25 gm icing sugar
- A 21 cm square cake tin, greased with butter,
- A wooden spoon (or electric cake mixer if you have one and an adult to help you use it),
- A large mixing bowl
- Tracing paper
- A sharp knife – and again an adult to help you use it.

- 200 gm soft margarine or butter
- 4 large eggs 250 gm soft ready to roll black icing
- 1 tube red writing icing
- 2 tablespoons of apricot jam

- A rolling pin
- A cooling tray.

NOW WASH YOUR PAWS BEFORE YOU START

THIS IS WHAT YOU DO:

The oven needs to be set to 180° / 160° fan/350° / Gas mark 4

Put the caster sugar and margarine into the mixing bowl and beat together with the wooden spoon (or electric mixer) until it is pale and fluffy.

Stir in the eggs and flour and keep beating the mixture until there are no lumps (Not even little ones!) and the mixture is smooth and creamy.

Now put the mixture into the baking tin and smooth the top with the back of the spoon.

Bake this in the oven for 55 to 60 minutes then take it out and leave it to cool in the tin for a few minutes before turning the cake out onto a cooling tray and leaving it until it is completely cold.

Sprinkle a little icing sugar onto your worktop and also onto the rolling pin then roll out the white icing sugar into a 21 cm square (Use the cake tin as a guide).

Now roll the black icing into an 8cm x 14 cm rectangle.

Spread the jam over the top of the cake, (This will help the icing to stick) then gently lay the white icing sugar square over the cake and press it down gently.

Copy or trace the outline of the black cat (see next page) onto the black icing sugar and carefully cut round the shape with a sharp knife.

Stick the black cat shape onto your cake with a few drops of water. Use the writing icing to draw the features (nose, eyes and mouth) onto the cat.

Finish the decorating by writing

HAPPY BIRTHDAY round the edge.

Get ready for the person you have made the cake for to be impressed you have made the cake!

...and don't forget to get some candles to put on top.

Samson
SHOWS YOU

Happy
Birthday

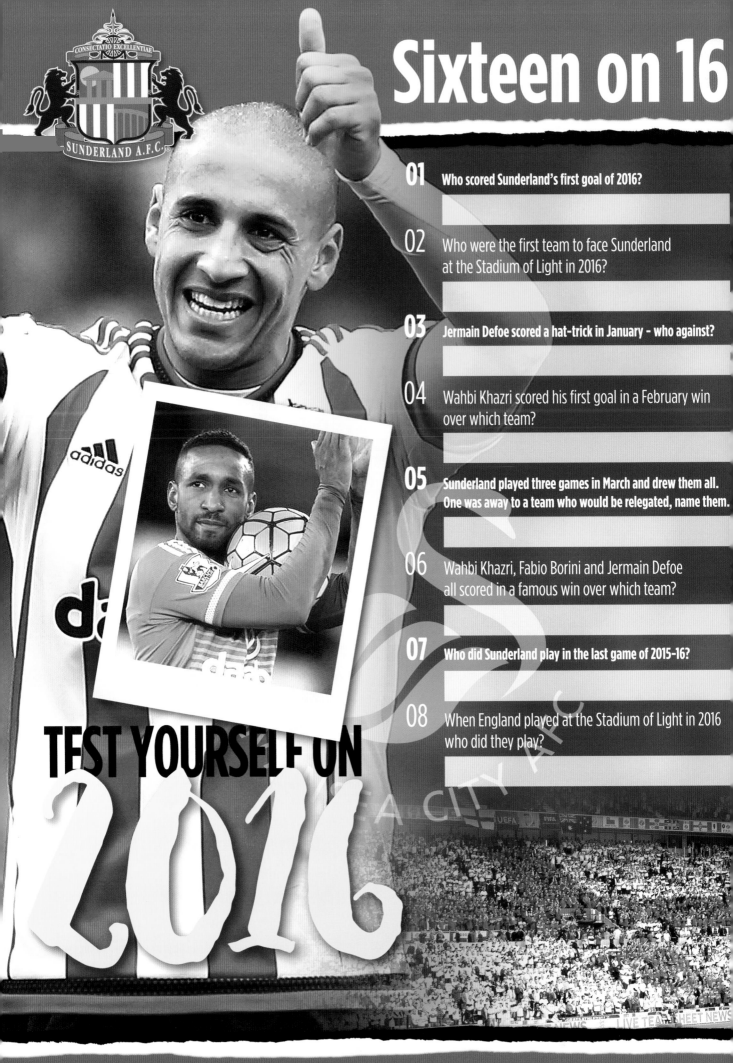

Sixteen on 16

01 Who scored Sunderland's first goal of 2016?

02 Who were the first team to face Sunderland at the Stadium of Light in 2016?

03 Jermain Defoe scored a hat-trick in January – who against?

04 Wahbi Khazri scored his first goal in a February win over which team?

05 Sunderland played three games in March and drew them all. One was away to a team who would be relegated, name them.

06 Wahbi Khazri, Fabio Borini and Jermain Defoe all scored in a famous win over which team?

07 Who did Sunderland play in the last game of 2015-16?

08 When England played at the Stadium of Light in 2016 who did they play?

TEST YOURSELF ON 2016

09 What do these numbers have in common:
5, 10, 20, 21, 24, 33 & 38?

10 Who was Sunderland's Young Player of the Year
for 2015-16?

11 Who was Sunderland's Player of the Year for 2015-16?

12 Which famous German team did SAFC draw with
in their final pre-season friendly before this season?

13 Who did Sunderland play in their first home game
of this season?

14 Who was the first player signed after David Moyes
took over as manager?

15 Who scored Sunderland's first goal of the 2016-17 season?

16 What was the score when Sunderland visited
Southampton at the end of August?

ANSWERS ON PAGE 62

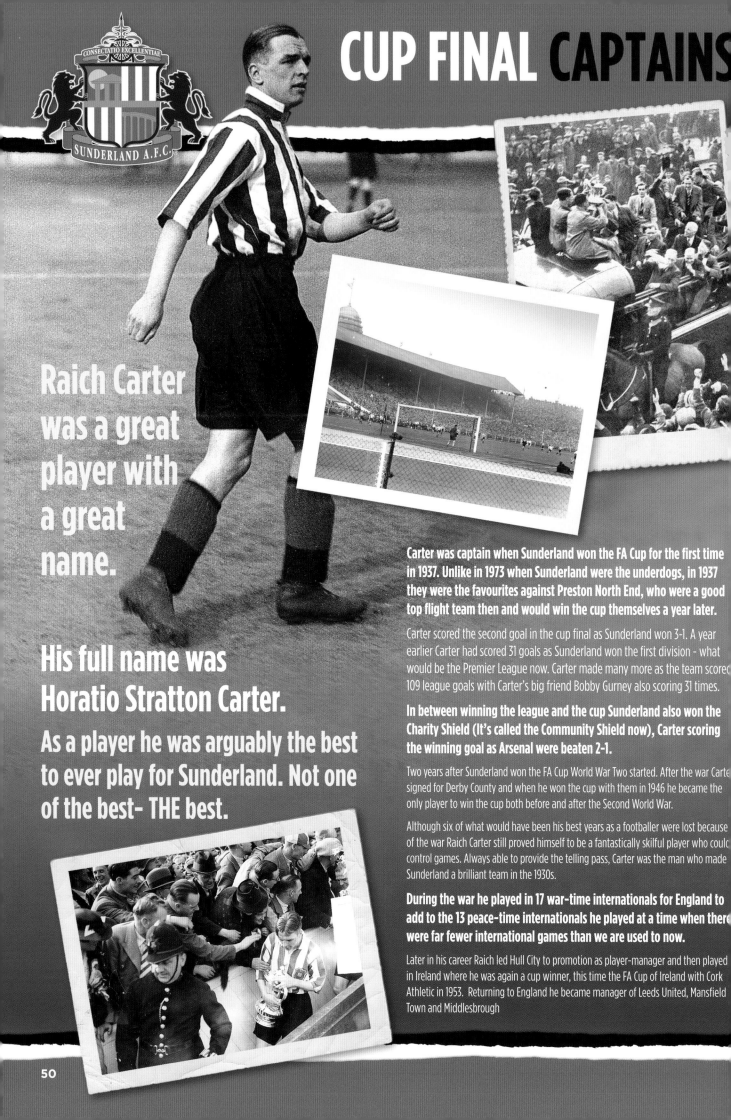

CUP FINAL CAPTAINS

Raich Carter was a great player with a great name.

His full name was Horatio Stratton Carter.

As a player he was arguably the best to ever play for Sunderland. Not one of the best- THE best.

Carter was captain when Sunderland won the FA Cup for the first time in 1937. Unlike in 1973 when Sunderland were the underdogs, in 1937 they were the favourites against Preston North End, who were a good top flight team then and would win the cup themselves a year later.

Carter scored the second goal in the cup final as Sunderland won 3-1. A year earlier Carter had scored 31 goals as Sunderland won the first division - what would be the Premier League now. Carter made many more as the team scored 109 league goals with Carter's big friend Bobby Gurney also scoring 31 times.

In between winning the league and the cup Sunderland also won the Charity Shield (It's called the Community Shield now), Carter scoring the winning goal as Arsenal were beaten 2-1.

Two years after Sunderland won the FA Cup World War Two started. After the war Carter signed for Derby County and when he won the cup with them in 1946 he became the only player to win the cup both before and after the Second World War.

Although six of what would have been his best years as a footballer were lost because of the war Raich Carter still proved himself to be a fantastically skilful player who could control games. Always able to provide the telling pass, Carter was the man who made Sunderland a brilliant team in the 1930s.

During the war he played in 17 war-time internationals for England to add to the 13 peace-time internationals he played at a time when there were far fewer international games than we are used to now.

Later in his career Raich led Hull City to promotion as player-manager and then played in Ireland where he was again a cup winner, this time the FA Cup of Ireland with Cork Athletic in 1953. Returning to England he became manager of Leeds United, Mansfield Town and Middlesbrough

1937

RAICH Carter

ANSWERS ON PAGE 62

SUNDERLAND A.F.C.

If you know who the mystery player is...

after one clue you get **5** points,

...after two clues you get **4** points,

...after three clues you get **3** points,

...after four clues you get **2** points,

...or after five clues you get **1** point.

There are a maximum 15 points available.
How many points will you get?

MYSTERY MAN A

1. Before signing for Sunderland he had played against Chelsea and Manchester City in the Champions League.
2. In the past he has been coached by Jurgen Klopp.
3. He has been a teammate of Leicester's Christian Fuchs at two different clubs.
4. He made his Sunderland debut as a sub at Spurs in January 2016.
5. He was signed from Bayern Munich

MYSTERY MAN B

1. He was born on the French island of Corsica.
2. He scored his first two goals for Sunderland against Manchester United and Chelsea.
3. Before joining SAFC he played in France for Bastia and Bordeaux.
4. He played for France at U21 level
5. He became a full international with Tunisia.

AM I

MYSTERY MAN C

1. He was born in Paris.
2. He played for Chateauroux and Lorient in France before joining Sunderland.
3. He represented France at U17, U18, U19 and U20 level.
4. He became a full international with Ivory Coast.
5. He scored twice for Sunderland against Everton in May in the game that secured the Lads' place in the Premier League.

Sunderland are in the Premier League for a tenth successive season this year and for that a lot of the credit has to go to the 2016 Player of the Year Jermain Defoe.

What a season the striker had. His goals secured many points at a time when each point was extremely valuable. He got the winner in the game of the season as Chelsea were beaten at the Stadium of Light in a critical victory a week before the end of the campaign. Seven days earlier he'd popped in a vital injury time equaliser at Stoke and of course amongst his other goals was one that put Sunderland in the lead at Newcastle.

Altogether Defoe scored 18 goals last season, 15 of them in the Premier League where he was the third highest English goal-scorer, behind only Harry Kane and Jamie Vardy, who both played for top three sides where forwards can expect many more chances than a player in a team near the bottom.

As well as his league goals, Jermain scored a hat-trick in the 6-3 Capital One Cup win over Exeter City at the Stadium of Light, and he earned himself another match ball later in the season when bagging three goals in a big 4-2 Premier League win at Swansea.

Jermain's goals made the difference when it came to keeping Sunderland up. No other team in the fight at the foot of the table had a consistent striker. In addition to Defoe's ability to regularly get his name on the score-sheet Jermain led by example with his contribution to the team. While Defoe is as good a goal-poacher as there is in the game this doesn't mean he is just a goal-hanger waiting for his team-mates to lay chances on a plate for him.

The Londoner got stuck in and worked hard for the side, putting in a shift every time so the rewards that came his way had certainly been worked for.

To be a Player of the Year obviously you have had an outstanding season and Jermain Defoe can take his place amongst the many great footballers who have been Sunderland's Player of the Year.

PLAYERS OF THE YEAR

YOUNG PLAYER OF THE YEAR

Duncan Watmore was Sunderland's Young Player of the Year in 2016. The England U21 international gave Sunderland a fresh young attacking option, which was always a valuable weapon. Having scored Sunderland's first home goal of the season against Norwich, Duncan quickly added a cup goal in the big win over Exeter, netted in the win over Stoke and wrapped up the crucial late season win over Norwich.

That goal at Carrow Road came on Duncan's comeback after 10 weeks out through injury. When he was hurt it was thought he would be out for the rest of the season but many dedicated hours of rehabilitation meant that the youngster returned to fitness much earlier than anticipated. His hard work meant he was able to add to Big Sam's options at the business end of the season and help keep Sunderland up.

The fans love Duncan's work rate and directness. He can scare the life out of defences and has the sort of enthusiasm for the game that people love to see.

LADIES PLAYER AND YOUNG PLAYER OF THE YEAR

Sunderland Ladies had an excellent campaign in their first year in the Women's Super League 1. Striker Beth Mead had a sensational season, pushing her way into the England set-up and becoming Sunderland Ladies' Player of the Year as well as winning the national PFA Young Player of the Year award.

England youth international forward Abbey Joice also had a first rate introduction to WSL1 and took the honour of being named Sunderland Ladies Young Player of the Year.

Until you're good enough to get into Sunderland's first team
(Keep practising — you never know, you might do it one day)
you can still get to see inside Sunderland's dressing room!

INTO THE Light

OUTSIDE THE
MONTGOMERY
SUITE.

THE MONTGOMERY SUITE

ON THE STAIRCASE
LEADING TO THE
DRESSING ROOMS

TAKE YOUR SEAT IN AN
EXECUTIVE BOX – POSH!

TAKE YOUR SEATS IN THE DRESSING ROOM

YOU CAN PRETEND YOU'RE THE MANAGER
AND SIT WHERE DAVID MOYES SITS WHEN SPEAKING
TO NEWSPAPER JOURNALISTS AFTER A MATCH

All you need to do is go on a stadium tour which will let you see parts of the stadium that you don't see when you are at the match.

Stadium tours take place at 1.30pm on weekdays and 2.00pm at weekends but do not happen on a day a match is on. You meet in the main entrance of the Stadium of Light and are taken around some of the most interesting places in the stadium. You get to see both dressing rooms, where the manager does his TV interviews, Quinn's bar, inside an executive box and best of all you get to run down the players' tunnel while the music plays!

There are loads of opportunities to take pictures and the tour guides are great at telling you about the history of the stadium. Stadium tours last as long as a match does and you get a special certificate to say you've taken the tour. It costs £10 for adults and £5 for over 65s and juniors while a family ticket for two adults and two children costs £25.

Once a month on a Friday there is also a special tour led by Jim Montgomery, the man who has played more games for Sunderland than anyone else ever has.

These cost £35 for adults and £18 for over 65s and juniors. People on this tour get a certificate and picture of Monty's famous cup final save, both signed by Jim and there's even a question and answer session and refreshments with Monty.

Any of these tours can be booked by calling tour manager Malcolm Hopkins on

0871 911 1224

SIT IN THE HOT-SEAT! THIS SUPPORTER KEEPS DAVID MOYES' SEAT WARM.

THIS TOUR GROUP TAKE THEIR PLACES IN THE DUG-OUT

YOU GET TO SEE INSIDE THE AWAY TEAM DRESSING ROOM AS WELL

TOUR GROUP LEADER STAN CARTER, ONE OF SIX GUIDES WHO LEAD THE STADIUM TOURS

RUN DOWN THE TUNNEL AND APPLAUD THE CROWD!

What was the first Sunderland kit you had?
Do you still have it? Have you got this season's?
Which year is your favourite Sunderland kit?
Do you get the new strip every season?

KIT

2010-11

The away kit for this season featured a cream coloured shirt and socks with maroon shorts. There was maroon on the top of the socks too and down the side of the shirts. Maroon and cream wasn't quite red and white, but it was close.

For lots of people the day the new strip comes out is as important as the day the fixtures are revealed. Take a look at the Sunderland kits we've pictured here and see which ones you like, and maybe which ones you've never seen before.

2016-17

This season's third kit is something very different for Sunderland. The pink & purple hoops are ultra modern.

2006-07

Ten years ago Sunderland wore an all light blue away kit with black flashes on the inner sleeves, collar and socks. The sponsor back then was Reg Vardy which was a local company that sold cars.